First Edition   2018

ISBN 978-7-5138-1614-4
Copyright 2018 by Sinolingua Co., Ltd
Published by Sinolingua Co., Ltd
24 Baiwanzhuang Road, Beijing 100037, China
Tel: (86) 10-68320585   68997826
Fax: (86) 10-68997826   68326333
http://www.sinolingua.com.cn
E-mail: hyjx@sinolingua.com.cn
Facebook: www.facebook.com/sinolingua
Printed by Beijing Xicheng Printing Co., Ltd

Printed in the People's Republic of China

前　言

中国是一个拥有灿烂文化的国度，无论是古代还是现代，都有许多智慧的人和智慧的事。"中国智慧故事汉语分级读物"就收集了这样一批闪烁着智慧光芒的有趣故事，题材涉及名人智慧、探案斗智、军事或商战谋略，以及科技创新等。我们根据非母语汉语学习者的阅读需求，用浅显明白、难度分级的汉语把它们一一呈现出来。让读者在学习汉语的同时，享受脑力激荡的乐趣。

"中国智慧故事汉语分级读物"以中学阶段及以上的汉语学习者为主要读者对象。这套读物根据语言难度划分为三个级别，每级包含若干分册，每册讲述一个中国古代或现代的智慧故事。其中1级为300词，故事长约2500字；2级为400词，故事长约3500字；3级为550词，故事长约4500字。构成故事的词汇均来源于HSK等语言标准（详见下表）。

级别	1级	2级	3级
对应级别	HSK1~2 CEFR A1-A2	HSK2~3 CEFR A2-B1	HSK3 CEFR A2-B1
词汇量	300	400	550
字数	2500	3500	4500

为了帮助读者适度地扩大词汇量，每个故事还将出现一定数量的生词，我们对这些生词进行了注音和英文释义，并给出了以应用为主的中文例句。为了方便教师检测汉语教学的效果，我们特别根据 IB 中文考试的新大纲编写了阅读理解练习题，附在每个故事之后。同时，每册读物均配有 24 幅生动的插图，这些图片不仅穿插在行文当中，而且还会作为"情节预告"出现在故事的正文之前。图片的巧妙呈现不仅使阅读更加轻松有趣，同时也为教师围绕图片实施教学任务提供了便利条件。读者通过阅读本系列读物，不仅能够迅速地掌握大量常用汉语语料，而且能够稳定地提高阅读理解及口语表达的能力。

要想稳步提高阅读水平，课内精读与课外泛读相结合是行之有效的方法之一。"中国智慧故事汉语分级读物"不仅是汉语学习者在课余进行泛读的好朋友，更是汉语教师在课堂上进行阅读教学的好帮手。读故事，学语言，长智慧——"中国智慧故事汉语分级读物"愿与大家在汉语学习的道路上快乐同行！

韩　颖　刘小琳

Preface

China is a country that boasts a diverse culture and enduring civilization. Inspirational stories replete with wisdom can be found throughout her history. Wisdom in Stories: Graded Chinese Readers is a series of carefully selected and entertaining stories that touch on many subjects. These include exceptional moments in the lives of renowned people, detective tactics, military and business strategies, and even innovations in science and technology. The stories are narrated in simple and concise language that is graded by reading difficulty into different levels to meet the learning needs of non-native speakers of the Chinese language. This approach enables readers to enjoy the clever twists and turns of these engaging stories while improving their Chinese.

Wisdom in Stories: Graded Chinese Readers is designed for Chinese learners who are at a middle school or higher level. Each title in this series focuses on one story from contemporary or ancient China, and is graded on a three-level system based on HSK and other established standards. For level 1, the expected Chinese vocabulary of the reader is 300 Chinese words while the total character count for each story is around 2,500. In level 2, the reader is expected to have a grasp of 400 Chinese words while the total character count for each story is around 3,500. For level 3, the numbers are 550 and 4,500 respectively. (See the table below for details.)

Level	1	2	3
Reference Standard	HSK1~2 CEFR A1-A2	HSK2~3 CEFR A2-B1	HSK3 CEFR A2-B1
Vocabulary Words	300	400	550
Character Count	2,500	3,500	4,500

To enable readers to gradually enrich their vocabulary, a limited number of new words are introduced in each story. These are accompanied by pinyin and English translation. In addition, example sentences are also provided to illustrate their usage. After each story, there are also reading exercises designed according to the latest IB Syllabus for Chinese. Instructors and independent learners can use them to assess reading comprehension. Twenty-four vivid and dynamic illustrations also help enhance the plot and serve as a "trailer" for each story. In addition to improving learners' reading experience, the illustrations can be used to design picture-based teaching tasks. Readers will benefit from diverse authentic Chinese texts featuring everyday language that will enable them to steadily increase their skills in reading and speaking.

The combination of intensive reading in class and extensive reading after class is an effective way to develop one's reading skills. Wisdom in Stories: Graded Chinese Readers can serve in both capacities and be of great use to both Chinese language learners and teachers. Stories, language and wisdom — this series hopes to accompany you on an enjoyable journey of learning Chinese.

Han Ying and Liu Xiaolin

背景和人物简介
Background and Characters

王法官（Wáng Fǎguān）：中国北方一个小县城的法官。
Judge Wang: A judge working in a small county in northern China.

谭财（Tán Cái）：肉店老板。
Tan Cai: Owner of a butcher's shop.

李二（Lǐ Èr）：卖柴的年轻人。
Li Er: A young firewood seller.

聪明① 的法官②

民国③时期，北方有一个小县城。有一年，城里来了一个姓王的新法官。别的法官上任④都是坐着好车，有很多人开路，但王法官跟别人不一样。

① 聪明 cōngmíng *adj.* clever; bright
e.g., 他从小就很聪明。
② 法官 fǎguān *n.* judge
e.g., 法官为这个案子很头疼。
③ 民国 mínguó *n.* Republic of China (1912-1949)
e.g., 民国时期一般指从1912年起，到1949年止。
④ 上任 shàngrèn *v.* take office
e.g., 新官上任三把火。

王法官让妻子和孩子坐在毛驴①上，自己②赶③毛驴。他一边赶路，一边了解④老百姓⑤的生活。

① 毛驴 máolǘ *n.* donkey
e.g., 小毛驴真可爱。
② 自己 zìjǐ *pron.* oneself
e.g., 你自己怎么看这个问题？
③ 赶 gǎn *v.* move; drive
e.g., 那个人赶着一头牛。
④ 了解 liǎojiě *v.* understand
e.g., 你一点儿都不了解她。
⑤ 老百姓 lǎobǎixìng *n.* common people
e.g., 老百姓都说他是个好官。

一路上,王法官了解到,这个地方做买卖的人老是缺斤少两①;还了解到,这里的警察②们常常欺压③老百姓。聪明的他决定改变这种风气。

在上任后的第一个赶集日,王法官穿上便服④,到集市⑤上去走走。他看见有一个地方围⑥了不少人,就过去看看有什么事。

① 缺斤少两 quējīn-shǎoliǎng
give short weight
e.g., 那个老板卖东西总是缺斤少两。

② 警察 jǐngchá n.
policeman; bailiff
e.g., 警察抓住了坏人。

③ 欺压 qīyā v. bully
e.g., 这个财主欺压百姓。

④ 便服 biànfú n. everyday clothes
e.g., 不要穿工作服,穿便服。

⑤ 集市 jíshì n. market
e.g., 我要去城里最大的集市。

⑥ 围 wéi v. surround
e.g., 大家纷纷围上去看。

王法官走近一看，是一个肉店①老板②正在和一个小伙子③吵架④，小伙子手里还拿着一小块牛肉⑤。

① 肉店 ròudiàn n.
butcher's shop
e.g., 你去肉店买二斤肉。
② 老板 lǎobǎn n.
shopkeeper
e.g., 我的老板住在我家旁边。
③ 小伙子 xiǎohuǒzi n.
young fellow
e.g., 他已经不是一个小伙子了。
④ 吵架 chǎojià v. quarrel
e.g., 你不要和别人吵架。
⑤ 牛肉 niúròu n. beef
e.g., 老王在卖牛肉。

<u>王法官</u>把小伙子拉出来,问他:"小伙子,这里发生了什么事?"

小伙子生气地说:"今天我来城里卖柴火①,卖了八角②钱。老母亲想吃肉,我就用五角钱买了二斤③肉。"

① 柴火 cháihuo *n.* firewood
e.g., 他点着了柴火。
② 角 jiǎo *m.w.* jiao
fractional unit of Chinese currency equaling 0.1 yuan
e.g., 西瓜一斤五角钱。
③ 斤 jīn *n. jin*, unit of weight equaling 0.5 kg
e.g., 苹果一斤三块钱。

"回去后我用朋友的秤①称②了一下,这二斤肉就少了半斤。我来肉店找他们,可是老板不认账③,还让人打我!"

王法官说:"小伙子,你不要跟他们生气。你为什么不去告④他呢?"

① 秤 chèng n. steelyard
e.g., 我已经踩坏三个体重秤了。
② 称 chēng v. weigh
e.g., 帮我称一下这条鱼。
③ 认账 rènzhàng v. admit what one has done
e.g., 爸爸问儿子是不是他干的,儿子就是不认账。
④ 告 gào v. sue
e.g., 我要去告你!

小伙子说:"这样的事太多了,法官会管①吗?"

王法官说:"会的。"

小伙子想了想,说:"可是,我不会写诉状②呀!"

王法官说:"你放心,不会写,可以说呀。"

小伙子高兴地说:"好,那我就去告他。"

① 管 guǎn v. subject sb to discipline
e.g., 你好好管管你家孩子!
② 诉状 sùzhuàng n. indictment
e.g., 他把诉状交给了法官。

王法官问:"你知道怎么告状吗?"

小伙子低下头说:"不知道。"

王法官说:"那我告诉你。你在法院①外面大声喊'冤枉'②,就有人出来带你进去。到了里面,不许看法官。法官问你什么,你就回答什么。"

小伙子说:"好的,我记住了,谢谢大哥!"说完,二人就告别③了。

① 法院 fǎyuàn *n.* court of law
e.g., 法院公开审理了这个案子。
② 冤枉 yuānwang *v.*
do someone injustice
e.g., 我们要小心,不要冤枉好人。
③ 告别 gàobié *v.*
bid farewell to
e.g., 我们在公园门口告别。

小伙子拿着肉来到法院门外,大叫"冤枉"。一个警察走出来,把他带了进去。小伙子远远看见法官,赶紧低下头。王法官就问:"你叫什么名字?家住在哪里?告的是什么人?"

小伙子低着头说:"大人,我叫李二,是李家庄人。我告的是肉店老板谭财。他的肉店缺斤少两,我买了二斤肉,就少给了半斤。我去找他说明白,他不但不认账,还让人打了我!"

王法官问:"真有这样的事?"

李二回答说:"真的!"

王法官问:"没有一句谎话①?"

李二说:"是的,没有一句谎话!"

王法官说:"我知道了。把肉店老板谭财带上来!"

不一会儿,肉店老板谭财就被警察带了上来。

① **谎话** huǎnghuà *n.* lie
e.g., 我们不能说谎话。

王法官问:"你是肉店的老板谭财吗?"

谭财说:"是,大人。"

王法官问:"你卖的肉多少钱一斤?"

谭财说:"两角五分一斤。"

王法官问:"五角该给多少肉?"

谭财说:"该给二斤。"

王法官说:"拿秤来!"警察拿来一杆秤。

王法官说:"你来称称这块肉有多重。"谭

财拿秤一称那块肉，二斤差了半斤。

王法官生气地说："你这坏人！二斤差半斤，一年你得少给人多少肉？这怎么可以！你是愿意赔① 钱，还是愿意关门？愿意赔钱就拿出五十块，愿意关门就不要再做生意了。"

谭财害怕② 地说："我愿意赔钱。"

① 赔 péi v. compensate
e.g., 他赔了她一辆自行车。
② 害怕 hàipà v. fear
e.g., 我害怕老鼠。

王法官说："好的，你去拿五十块钱来，以后不能再这样做了。"

谭财说："是，大人。"说完他赶紧① 离开了法院，不一会儿就拿来了五十块钱。

① 赶紧 gǎnjǐn adv.
without delay
e.g., 你赶紧去吧！

王法官对李二说:"这五十块钱给你,回去做个小买卖,照顾你的老母亲吧。"

李二没想到王法官会把这五十块钱都给他,又惊又喜,抬头一看,原来①王法官就是让他来告状的那个大哥!李二赶紧道谢②。

① 原来 yuánlái adv.
as it turns out
e.g., 原来你也是北京人啊!
② 道谢 dàoxiè v. thank
e.g., 我要当面向他道谢。

王法官对李二说:"你拿着这么多钱不安全,我让人送你回家吧。"

王法官叫来两个警察,对他们说:"你们俩送李二回家。"两个警察就带着李二出了门。

两个警察边走边想:一个卖柴的,白白得了五十块钱,真是太让人眼红① 了。

① 眼红 yǎnhóng v.
be jealous
e.g., 不要看到别人挣了大钱就眼红。

两个警察互相①看了一下，都知道了对方的意思。一个警察对李二说："你今天一点儿不费力②，白白得了五十块钱。你看我们五个警察天天辛辛苦苦，一个月才挣③十块钱。今天你得了这么多钱，还不分我们点儿，让我们每人买双靴子④。"

① 互相 hùxiāng adv. each other
e.g., 同学之间要互相帮助。

② 费力 fèilì v. need great effort
e.g., 这个工作很费力。

③ 挣 zhèng v. earn
e.g., 我想快点儿长大挣钱。

④ 靴子 xuēzi n. boots
e.g., 冬天穿靴子。

李二没办法,只好说:"好吧,你们要多少呢?"

另一个警察说:"你拿出二十五块给我们吧,剩下的二十五块给你。"

李二拿出二十五块给了两个警察。到了西城门,两个警察又商量① 了一下,一个警察说:"那二十五块大家分,咱们每个人只能分得五块钱,这个卖柴的还有二十五块呢。"

① 商量 shāngliang v. discuss
e.g., 有什么事儿你跟我商量。

另一个警察说:"这样吧,咱们再问他要十块。"

这两个人追上前面走的李二,说:"李二,今后你还想进城来办事儿吗?"

李二说:"我怎么能不来呢?"

一个警察说:"那就好。你还有二十五块,也是白得的。我们送你走了这么远的路,你还得再给我们一些钱。"

李二说:"我给了你们二十五块,你们已经有买靴子的钱了。"

另一个警察说:"那不行,你还得再给我们十块。要不然,以后你进城办事,会有麻烦。"

李二想:警察不能得罪①,再给他们十块吧,我还有十五块呢。于是,李二又给了他们十块钱。

这两个警察拿到钱后就走了。

① 得罪 dézuì v. **offend**
e.g., 我什么时候得罪过你?

李二继续往家走。走了一段时间，又有两个警察追过来，说："李二你站住！"

李二想，我手里的这十五块也剩①不下了，就说："二位老爷②，我只剩下十五块了，全都给你们吧。"

这两个警察说："法官大人让我们把你带回法庭去！"

到了法庭，王法官问："李二，那五十块

① 剩 shèng v. **be left over**
e.g., 我手里没剩多少钱了。
② 老爷 lǎoye n.
master; lord
e.g., 请青天大老爷给我做主啊！

钱呢?拿出来我看看。"

李二一想,坏了,先分了二十五块,后又被要去了十块,我只剩下十五块了,怎么拿得出来呢?他只好说:"大人,我拿不出来。"

王法官问:"怎么拿不出来?"

李二说:"我不敢说。"

王法官说:"你不说,就打你!"

李二没有办法,就把刚才的经过①都说了。

王法官想,听人说这里的警察经常欺压百姓,

① 经过 jīngguò n.
course; process
e.g., 你把事情的经过再说一遍。

今天看来果然是这样。连我法官给的钱他们也敢敲诈①,就知道他们平时是怎么对待百姓的了。

想到这儿,王法官说:"分到李二的钱的警察,都站出来!"

得到钱的警察都害怕地站了出来。王法官很生气地说:"你们敲诈勒索②,欺压百姓,每人罚十块,共五十块。"

王法官又指着送李二到西城门的那两个警察说:"你们俩两次敲诈李二,每人再多罚

① 敲诈 qiāozhà v. blackmail
e.g., 敲诈是犯罪。
② 勒索 lèsuǒ v. extort
e.g., 他的钱被勒索了。

十块！所有钱全部交给李二！"

五个警察把钱给了李二后，王法官对李二说："你可以回家了。要是再有人向你要钱，你就回来告诉我！"

李二感谢了法官后，回家去了。

原来，王法官是故意让那两个警察送李二回家的。他猜到这两个警察会敲诈李二，所以想借这个机会改变①县城的不良②风气③。

从那以后，这个小县城里做买卖的人们再也不敢缺斤少两，警察们再也不敢敲诈老百姓了。

① 改变 gǎibiàn v.
change; alter
e.g., 你不可能改变他。
② 不良 bùliáng adj.
bad; unhealthy
e.g., 我消化不良。
③ 风气 fēngqì n.
established practice
e.g., 这儿的风气不好。

A Clever Judge

The story happened in a small county during the period of Republic of China. One year in the county, there was to be a new judge surnamed Wang. Other judges would ride in a sedan car surrounded by many people when taking office, but Wang was not like them.

Instead, he asked his wife and child to mount a donkey. He drove the donkey and traveled incognito to the office while getting a view of local life along the way.

Wang came to understand that merchants in the region tended to short their customers on weight, and that the policemen would often bully the folks. The clever judge made up his mind to change the malpractice.

On the first market day after taking office, Wang spent time at the market in his casual wear. When he noticed a sea of people gathering around an area, he went over to see what was going on.

Wang got in for a closer look. He found a butcher arguing with a young man holding a small piece of beef.

Wang pulled the youngster out of the crowd and asked,"Young

man, what's the matter here?"

The youngster answered angrily, "Today I came to town and sold firewood for eight *jiao*. My old mother wanted some beef, so I spent five *jiao* on two *jin*."

"After getting home, I used my friend's scale to weigh it. I found that it was short by half a *jin*. So I came to complain, but the butcher refused to admit it. He even told someone to beat me."

Wang said, "Young man, don't be angry with them. Why don't you go to court instead?"

The youngster answered, "Alas! This kind of problem happens so much. Will the judge really attend to it?"

Wang answered, "Yes, he will."

However, the youngster hesitated, saying, "But, I can't even write an indictment."

Wang replied, "Rest assured. You need not write anything, you can speak it."

The youngster was happy. "Okay then, I will sue him."

Wang asked, "Do you know how to bring a lawsuit against someone?"

The youngster lowered his head ."I don't."

Wang said,"I can tell you. You shout 'I am wronged!' outside the court, then someone will come to bring you in. Answer every question the judge asks, but don't ever look at him."

The youngster answered,"Okay, I've got it. Thanks a lot."
Then they parted.

The youngster went to the court taking the beef with him and began to cry foul. A bailiff came out to take him in. He saw the judge in the distance and quickly lowered his head. Wang asked, "What is your name? Where do you live? Who are you suing?"

The youngster answered looking down,"Sir, my name is Li Er. I am from Lijiazhuang Village. I want to sue Tan Cai, owner of the butcher's shop. He is shorting customers on weight. I bought two *jin* of beef, and half was missing. I went to clear it up, but he wouldn't admit it. He even sent someone to beat me."

Wang asked, "Is this true?"

Li Er replied, "Yes."

Wang asked, "Not a single lie?"

Li Er answered, "No, not a single lie."

Wang then said, "I see. Bring Tan Cai up."

After a short while, Tan Cai was brought up.

Judge Wang asked, "Are you Tan Cai?"

Tan Cai answered, "Yes, Sir."

Wang asked, "For how much do you sell beef per *jin*?"

Tan Cai replied, "Two *jiao* and five *fen* per *jin*."

Wang asked, "How much beef should you give for five *jiao*?"

Tan Cai answered, "Two *jin*."

Wang ordered, "Bring a steelyard here." A bailiff fetched a steelyard.

Wang said, "You measure how heavy the meat is." Tan Cai weighed the beef. It was half a *jin* short of two *jin*.

Judge Wang was angry. "You're a bad man. Half a *jin* for two *jin*, then how much beef do you short your customers per year? How dare you? Which do you prefer, a compensation or shutdown? The compensation will be 50 *yuan* or you have to close your business.

Tan Cai was scared. "I'd prefer a compensation."

Wang said, "Good. Go and get 50 *yuan* and promise you won't do this again."

Tan Cai replied, "Yes, Sir." Saying this, he rushed away and after a while brought back 50 *yuan*.

Wang told Li Er, "Take the 50 *yuan*, go back to start a small business and take care of your old mother."

Li Er did not expect to get 50 *yuan*. Surprised and delighted, he looked up only to find the judge was none other than the one who had encouraged him to come to the court. Li Er hastened to thank him.

The judge said to Li, "It's not safe for you to take so much money home. I will ask someone to send you." He called for two bailiffs, saying, "You two take Li Er home." The two bailiffs then left with Li Er.

The two bailiffs thought on the way: how enviable it is for a firewood seller to gain 50 *yuan* for nothing.

The two exchanged glances and knew what the other was thinking. One of them said to Li Er, "You got 50 *yuan* today without any effort. All five of us work hard every day and each earns only ten *yuan* a month. You got so much money today and should share it with all of us so that we can buy ourselves a pair of boots."

Li Er could do nothing but say, "Okay. How much do you want?"

The other said, "You give us 25 *yuan* and keep the rest."

Li Er gave them 25 *yuan*. Arriving at the West City Gate, the two bailiffs slowed down to whisper for a while. One said to the other, "25 *yuan* for five people. That's just five per person. This firewood seller still has 25 *yuan*."

The other said, "Therefore, we should ask him for ten *yuan* more."

Then they caught up with Li Er and asked, "Li Er, are you going to come to town for business in the future?"

Li Er replied, "How can't I come?"

One bailiff said, "That's right. You've still gained 25 *yuan* with no effort. We have walked such a long distance with you. You should give us more money."

Li Er replied, "I have given you 25 *yuan*. You already have enough money to buy boots."

The other said, "No, it won't do. You should give us ten *yuan* more. Otherwise, you will get into trouble in the future when you do business in town."

Li Er reckoned: I shouldn't offend the bailiffs. Give them ten *yuan* and I will still have 15 *yuan*. So Li Er gave the two bailiffs ten *yuan*.

They took the money and left.

As Li Er walked on, another two bailiffs ran to him saying, "Li Er, don't move."

Li Er thought: the remaining 15 *yuan* will leave me now. He said, "Masters, I've got only 15 *yuan* left. Please take them all."

These two bailiffs said, "The judge told us to bring you back to the court."

At the court, Judge Wang asked, "Li Er, where are the 50 *yuan*? Show me."

Li Er was upset. First 25 *yuan* was given out, then ten *yuan*. How could he show 50 *yuan*? He replied, "Sir, I can't."

Wang asked, "Why can't you?"

Li Er replied, "I daren't say."

Wang said, "Speak or be beaten!"

Li Er had no way to avoid telling the whole story. The judge meditated on this: I heard the bailiffs often bullied the civilians. Now it's been proven true. They even dared extort what I had given out. It can now be seen what they do in everyday life.

Thinking of this, Wang said, "Those who got Li Er's money, show yourselves."

All the bailiffs who shared the money stood out in fear. The judge fell into a rage, "You blackmailed and bullied this civilian. Each of you will be fined ten *yuan*, a total of 50 *yuan*."

Pointing to the two bailiffs who had taken Li Er to the West City Gate, he said, "You two committed blackmail twice. Each will be fined ten *yuan* more. Give the money all to Li Er."

After the five bailiffs handed the fine to Li Er, Wang told him, "You may go home now. If other people ask for your money, you can come back to me."

Li Er thanked the judge and went home.

In fact, Judge Wang dispatched the two bailiffs on purpose to let them send Li home. He anticipated that the two might blackmail him along the way. The clever judge thus took the chance to curb the malpractice in the county.

From that time onwards, no businessmen dared give short weight and no policemen dared blackmail the common people in the small county.

课后练习题 Exercises

一 根据故事内容给下列各题选择一个正确的答案。
Choose the correct answer according to the story.

1. 王法官是怎么上任的？（　　）
   A. 坐着好车　　　　　B. 有很多人开路
   C. 自己赶着毛驴　　　D. 抱着孩子

2. 肉店老板少给了李二多少肉？（　　）
   A. 半两　　B. 一两　　C. 半斤　　D. 一斤

3. 王法官让肉店老板赔了李二多少钱？（　　）
   A. 10 块　　B. 10 块　　C. 25 块　　D. 50 块

4. 两个警察一共敲诈了李二多少钱？（　　）
   A. 10 块　　B. 15 块　　C. 35 块　　D. 50 块

5. 李二最后拿着多少钱回家了？（　　）
   A. 50 块　　B. 70 块　　C. 100 块　　D. 85 块

二 从故事的第二、三段中，找出与下列词语意思最接近的一个词语。

Find the synonyms of the following words in the second and third paragraph of the story.

例：美丽　　　漂亮

1. 老婆　　　_____
2. 打听　　　_____

三 根据故事，从下列选项中选出三个正确的叙述。

Choose three correct statements based on your understanding of the story.

A. 王法官是一个县的法官。

B. 谭财和李二吵架，是因为李二付的钱是假钱。

C. 王法官让小伙子去法院告状，还告诉小伙子自己就是法官，小伙子非常高兴。

D. 李二告赢了，谭财输了。

E. 王法官惩罚了敲诈勒索的警察们。

四 选词填空。
Choose the appropriate word to fill in the blanks.

王法官走近一看，是一个肉店老板正在和一个小伙子_____，小伙子手里还拿着一小块牛肉。

王法官把小伙子拉出来，问他："小伙子，这里_____了什么事？"

小伙子生气地说："今天我来城里卖柴火，卖了八角钱。老母亲想吃肉，我就用五角钱买了二斤肉。"

"回去后我用朋友的秤_____了一下，这二斤肉就_____了半斤。我来肉店找他们，可是老板不_____，还让人打我！"

A. 称　　B. 吵架　　C. 差
D. 认账　　E. 发生

看图说话：请用中文描述下面这张图片的内容，尽量说清人物、背景和事件经过，可以加上你自己对人物或事件的看法及评价。

Describe the following picture in Chinese, including the characters, background information and plot. You can also add your comments on the characters or the story.

 简答题。

Answer the following question succinctly.

王法官最后是怎么处理敲诈李二的警察的？

课后练习答案　Keys to the exercises

一、根据故事内容给下列各题选择一个正确的答案。
　　1. C　2. C　3. D　4. C　5. D

二、从故事的第二、三段中，找出与下列词语意思最接近的一个词语。
　　1. 妻子　　2. 了解

三、根据故事，从下列选项中选出三个正确的叙述。
　　A D E

四、选词填空。
　　B E A C D

五、看图说话。
　　答案略

六、简答题。
　　答案略

项目策划：刘小琳　韩　颖
责任编辑：李婷晓
英文编辑：薛彧威
插图绘制：硕果儿
封面设计：何思倩　牛慧珍

图书在版编目（CIP）数据

聪明的法官：汉英对照 / 吕明明改编；韩芙芸译. -- 北京：华语教学出版社，2018.8
（中国智慧故事汉语分级读物）
ISBN 978-7-5138-1614-4

Ⅰ. ①聪… Ⅱ. ①吕… ②韩… Ⅲ. ①汉语－对外汉语教学－语言读物 Ⅳ. ①H195.5

中国版本图书馆CIP数据核字（2018）第169986号

聪明的法官

吕明明　改编

韩芙芸　翻译

*

©华语教学出版社有限责任公司

华语教学出版社有限责任公司出版

（中国北京百万庄大街24号　邮政编码 100037）

电话: (86)10-68320585　68997826

传真: (86)10-68997826　68326333

网址：www.sinolingua.com.cn

电子信箱：hyjx@sinolingua.com.cn

北京玺诚印务有限公司印刷

2018年（32开）第1版

2018年第1版第1次印刷

（汉英）

ISBN 978-7-5138-1614-4

定价：16.90元